A Note to P

DK READERS is a compelling program for beginning readers, designed in conjunction with leading literacy experts, including Dr. Linda Gambrell, Director of the School of Education at Clemson University. Dr. Gambrell has served on the Board of Directors of the International Reading Association and as President of the National Reading Conference.

Beautiful illustrations and superb full-color photographs combine with engaging, easy-to-read stories to offer a fresh approach to each subject in the series. Each DK READER is guaranteed to capture a child's interest while developing his or her reading skills, general knowledge, and love of reading.

The four levels of DK READERS are aimed at different reading abilities, enabling you to choose the books that are exactly right for your child:

Level 1 – Beginning to read
Level 2 – Beginning to read alone
Level 3 – Reading alone
Level 4 – Proficient readers

The "normal" age at which a child begins to read can be anywhere from three to eight years old, so these levels are only a general guideline.

No matter which level you select, you can be sure that you are helping your child learn to read, then read to learn!

LONDON, NEW YORK, MUNICH,
MELBOURNE, AND DELHI

Project Editors Anna Lofthouse
and Caryn Jenner
Series Editor Deborah Lock
Senior Art Editor Cheryl Telfer
Project Art Editor Jacqueline Gooden
Art Editor Nicky Liddiard
U.S. Editor Elizabeth Hester
DTP Designer Almudena Diaz
Production Shivani Pandey
Jacket Designer Chris Drew
Indexer Lynn Bresler

Reading Consultant
Linda Gambrell, Ph.D.

First American Edition, 2003
03 04 05 10 9 8 7 6 5 4 3 2 1
Published in the United States by DK Publishing, Inc.
375 Hudson Street, New York, New York 10014

Published in Great Britain by Dorling Kindersley Limited

Library of Congress Cataloging-in-Publication Data
Hayden, Kate.
 Amazing buildings / by Kate Hayden.
 --1st American ed.
  p. cm. -- (Dorling Kindersley readers)
 Summary: Showcases such unusual buildings as Stadium Australia,
the Eiffel Tower, and the Roman Colosseum.
 ISBN 0-7894-9308-X -- ISBN 0-7894-9220-2 (pbk.).
 1. Buildings--Juvenile literature. 2. Architecture--Juvenile literature.
[1.Buildings. 2.Architecture.] I. Title. II. Dorling Kindersley readers.
NA2555. H39 2003
720'.9--dc21   2002073391

Color reproduction by Colourscan, Singapore
Printed and bound in China by L Rex Printing Co., Ltd.

The publisher would like to thank the following for their kind permission
to reproduce their images: c=center, a=above, b=below, l=left, r=right.
 2: Corbis: tr, br; 3: Corbis; 4: Getty Images/Image Bank bl;
5: ImageState tl, tr, cl, b; 6-7: Still Pictures; 11: Corbis t; 12: Corbis br;
13: Getty Images/Telegraph; 14-15: James Davis Travel Photography;
15: Corbis tr, Hutchison Library/John Hatt bc; 16: Corbis; 17: Corbis;
18: Corbis; 19: Getty Images/Image Bank br; 20: Getty Images/Stone;
21: Getty Images/Stone; 22: Corbis bl. 22-23: Powerstock Photolibrary;
24-5: Corbis; 25: ImageState c, Zefa tr; 26-7: Katz/FSP; 27: Agence
France Presse tr; 28: Apex Photo Agency/Simon Burt tl; 28-29:
alamy.com b, Zefa Picture Library t; 29: Apex Photo Agency/Simon cl;
30-31: NASA t; 32: Corbis tl, tr, cl, cr; 33: Corbis
 All other images © Dorling Kindersley
 For further information see: www.dkimages.com

See our complete product line at

www.dk.com

DK READERS

BEGINNING 2 TO READ ALONE

Amazing Buildings

Written by Kate Hayden

DK Publishing, Inc.

Imagine a building–
an amazing building.
Does your building stand up tall?
Or does it spread out **wide?**
Is your building new,
with lots of shiny windows?
Or is it old and made of stone?
Do you know how
buildings are made?

1) An architect draws plans and makes models to show what a building will look like.

2) Construction workers lay sturdy foundations in the ground.

3) They build the walls, leaving gaps for the windows and doors.

4) The roof is added, and then glass is put in the windows.

A big city like this has
all kinds of buildings.
There are tall buildings,
wide buildings, office buildings,
apartment buildings, and more.

There are weird and wonderful buildings all over the world. They are built to be both useful and fun to look at.

The pyramids in Egypt
were built over 4,000 years ago.
These monuments were made
as burial sites for
Egyptian kings and
their treasure.

To build the pyramids, workers had to drag heavy stones up a ramp, one by one.

Many hands
It took 4,000 men twenty years to build the biggest pyramid.

The pyramids were built to last for a long time.

The Ancient Romans built
a massive stadium called
the Colosseum.
The Romans were the first to
use concrete
to make
buildings.

The Colosseum was oval-shaped
and seated up to 50,000 people.
The Romans loved to watch trained
fighters, called gladiators,
battle each other.
Cheers and boos
from the crowd
made echoes
all around
the stadium.

This fairy-tale castle, perched on a craggy hilltop in Germany, is called Neuschwanstein (NOY-shvan-stine). Earlier castles were built to protect the people inside, who could spy on approaching enemies from the tall towers. But Neuschwanstein was built just to look beautiful.

A Disney castle
Does this castle look familiar? Cinderella's castle in Disneyland is modeled after Neuschwanstein Castle.

One of the world's biggest palaces
is at Versailles (ver-SY) in France.
It has over 2,000 windows,
1,200 fireplaces and 67 staircases.
There is also a Hall of Mirrors
at Versailles.

When the palace
was built 300 years ago,
mirrors were very rare.
Visitors were amazed
to see their reflections.

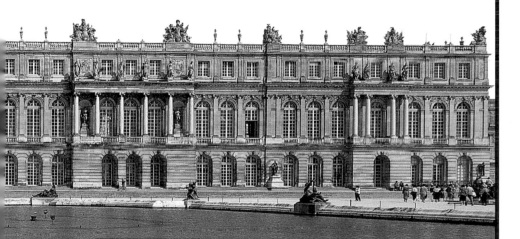

Fit for a King
The King's bedroom
was at the center
of the palace.
Louis XIV even
signed papers in bed!

The Eiffel Tower in Paris, France, is made of iron.

It was the tallest building in the world when it was built in 1889.

In those days it was unusual to make buildings out of metal. Since then, metal has been used to make buildings taller and taller.

Extra strength

The criss-cross pattern of the metal bars gives the Eiffel Tower extra strength and stability.

The tallest buildings of all
are called skyscrapers because
they seem to touch the sky.
The two Petronas Towers in
Malaysia are the tallest skyscrapers in
the world, at 1,483 feet (452 meters).
Each tower has 88 floors.
Visitors can walk
from one building
to the other on
the Skybridge.

It takes a whole
month to clean
all the windows
on one tower!

Some buildings have big, round roofs called domes.

The dome on Florence Cathedral in Italy was difficult to build.

Builders had to make another dome inside the cathedral to support the huge outer dome.

Workers walked through passages between the inner and outer domes.

The domes on
St. Basil's Cathedral
in Russia are called
onion domes.

Have you ever seen a building
in the shape of a ball?
The round building in this picture
is called Spaceship Earth.
It is at the Epcot Center
theme park in Florida.
Over 11,000 triangles cover
the surface to make it look
perfectly round and white—like
a huge golf ball!

More curves

This hotel in Dubai was
designed to look like a
wave. It has 600 rooms
for guests—all with
ocean views!

Think of the amazing shapes
of other modern buildings.
What do these buildings
look like to you?

The Sydney Opera House
in Australia looks like
the billowing sails
of a sailing boat.

The Guggenheim Museum in Spain may remind you of a large ship.

A gleaming roof
The roof of the Sydney Opera House is covered by over one million ceramic tiles.

Look at this huge stadium.
Stadium Australia was built for
the games of the 2000 Olympics.
It was designed to be friendly
to the environment.
This means it uses less electricity
for lights and air conditioning.

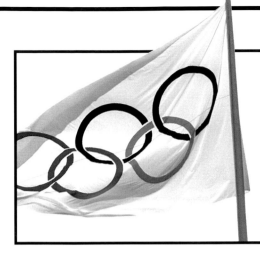

Olympics
New stadiums are often built for special events, such as the Olympic Games.

The stadium has big tanks to collect rainwater that falls on the roof. The rainwater is recycled to water the field or even to flush the toilets!

Where can you grow bananas indoors? In a giant greenhouse!

At the Eden Project in England, the latest technology is used to create habitats from around the world.

Even when it's cold and dry outside, the weather is hot and damp inside the Humid Tropics Biome.

Jungle plants grow as if they are in the middle of a rain forest.

One of the most
amazing modern
buildings is way
out in space.

All of the parts for the International Space Station come from Earth, on board the Space Shuttle. Who knows what other amazing buildings may be built in the future?

More building facts

A moat surrounds many castles, such as Raglan Castle in Great Britain. A moat is a ditch filled with water to keep enemies out.

The Ice Hotel in Canada is rebuilt every winter using fresh ice and snow. Every year, it looks different.

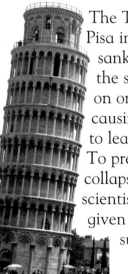

The Tower of Pisa in Italy sank into the soft soil on one side, causing it to lean. To prevent collapse, scientists have given it special supports.

The Great Wall of China was built to keep out invaders. It is so long that it can be seen from space.

The World Trade Center was a group of seven office buildings that opened in New York City in 1973. Two of these buildings were 110-story skyscrapers known as the twin towers—the tallest sights on the New York City skyline. On September 11, 2001, the twin towers and other buildings were destroyed in a terrorist attack.